FINDING LIGHT IN THE SHADOWS

SHADOWS

UNDERSTANDING AND PREVENTING SUICIDE

WISE KUKU

—INTRODUCTION—

I was born into a very disciplined family where tough love without question was the order. We lived by the rules and our co-habiting was characterised by routines. To an outsider, we looked like the perfect family where the parents and children had enviable attitudes but the soul distancing was oblivious to all. If only they knew what went on behind the doors. As a first child, high and unrealistic expectations were set for me to meet. Lack of understanding and thought for my feelings/emotions as a child irrespective of whatever circumstance and the reason I could not speak on my mistakes, issues and challenges affecting me without fear of being condemned made me fall into depression which is fast becoming popular among young people worldwide.

Depression is a complicated and multifaceted mental health illness that is characterized by a variety of symptoms such as a protracted grief, a lack of interest in routine activities, and an overwhelming sense of hopelessness. This is to say that when a youth begins to lose interest in doing his/her daily chores or begins to stay away from his friends; if he or she easily gets exhausted and discouraged, then depression may be setting in.

A major concern of depression is suicide which is a major cause of death in many countries and is a major health issue. It is important to recognize the signs of depression and take measures to prevent suicide. Depression can lead to feelings of hopelessness, helplessness, and worthlessness, which can make individuals more likely to take their own lives. In addition, understanding the complex interactions between depression, suicide, and environmental factors can help inform prevention strategies. Additionally, it is important to recognize the signs of depression so that individuals can be referred to professional help. Finally, it is important to create an environment where individuals feel supported and have access to the resources they need to cope with their depression.

Suicide is a deeply concerning and sensitive issue that affects millions of lives worldwide. It cuts through cultural, social, and economic boundaries, leaving devastating impacts on individuals, families, and communities. In this book, we will embark on a comprehensive journey to shed light on the complexities surrounding suicide and explore ways to address and prevent this heartbreaking crisis.

In a world marked by numerous challenges and complexities, there are few issues as deeply distressing and enigmatic as suicide. The human capacity for resilience and hope is vast, but it can be overshadowed by the darkness of despair. I am driven by an unswerving determination to address this deeply troubling aspect of our society and to contribute to its prevention.

The motivation behind this endeavor is multifaceted. First and foremost, my personal experiences and encounters with individuals affected by suicide have stirred within me an unwavering commitment to explore its intricacies. I have witnessed the heart-wrenching aftermath it leaves in its wake, not only for those who lose their lives but also for their loved ones who grapple with grief, guilt, and endless questions.

Furthermore, my background and life experiences have illuminated the dire need for a comprehensive and accessible resource on this topic. Suicide is an intricate, multi-dimensional issue that demands a nuanced understanding, and this book is a response to that demand. I firmly believe that knowledge is a powerful tool, and by enhancing our collective understanding of the underlying causes, warning signs, and preventative measures, we can make significant strides towards saving lives.

In writing this book, my foremost aim is to dismantle the shroud of silence and stigma surrounding suicide. I hope to foster open and compassionate dialogue that enables individuals, families, and communities to confront this issue without judgment or fear. Through meticulous research and the insights of experts in the field, I aspire to provide a well-informed perspective that aids in recognizing and addressing the signs of distress in ourselves and others.

Ultimately, I envision "Understanding and Prevention of Suicide" as a beacon of hope, a guide for those who seek answers, and a resource for those striving to make a difference. My aspiration is to empower readers with knowledge and practical tools to intervene, support, and prevent suicide, ensuring that fewer lives are lost to this tragic and preventable outcome.

As we embark on this journey together, my hope is that we collectively contribute to a world where the darkness of despair is met with the illumination of understanding and the warmth of compassion. May this book serve as a small but meaningful step towards a future where suicide is no longer a pervasive and devastating presence in our lives.

With profound dedication and a sincere commitment to change,
WISE KUKU

TABLE OF CONTENT

Chapter 1

THE GLOBAL CONCERN OF SUICIDE AND DEPRESSION

When we take time to examine the prevalence and consequences of suicide, we set the stage for an in-depth exploration of the psychological factors that contribute to suicidal thoughts and tendencies. Suicide can be described as "the deliberate act of causing one's own death" according to the English learners' dictionary. It is a complex phenomenon influenced by a multitude of factors such as social isolation, adverse life events, despair and mental health disorders like depression, bipolar disorder, schizophrenia, and anxiety disorders, substance abuse, access to lethal means, as well as cultural and religious beliefs.

It's crucial to emphasize that suicidal thoughts should never be underestimated. It could make a strong individual become emotionally damaged for the rest of his life. As a young man, I had contemplated suicide as the only option to get out of my miserable life which left me emotionally damaged.

Suicide is a deep issue that transcends geographical boundaries, impacting individuals of all ages, genders, and cultures. Shockingly, the World Health Organization (WHO) estimates that approximately

800,000 people succumb to suicide each year, making it a leading cause of death on a global scale. I once did a research on YouTube and found that one of the top findings people search for is "how to commit suicide." This is very alarming and disturbing; there's an urgent need to understand and address this pervasive problem that is fast gaining popularity among young people.

I remember a young man fell into depression on the grounds that the demands his parents placed on him as an only child were annoyingly unrealistic. He is from a middle-class family where he's expected to earn money at an early age to survive. His parents had invested their savings on giving him the best legacy- education and now, it was his turn to start repaying them, more like a return-on-investment scheme. As they say in a Nigerian parlance, "it's the breast of its child that a rat sucks at old age" which invariably translates to parents becoming the responsibility of their children when they perceive that the child has come of age. Usually, this role switch doesn't augur well with many young people in our generation who have not been taught or shown how to handle pressure.

When a child sees his poor parents struggle through their career just to pay school fees and meet family needs, he or she will naturally have a sense of compassion to do all he can to contribute his own quota to the retirement plan of his parents. However, this may create a pressure on the children to deliver. So, he/she strives to get good grades in order to get good jobs but it's not the same experience for an academically weak child who finds it very hard to cope up with studies while living under pressure to deliver because his parents have paid the fees through their nose.

The guy in question has had his grades nose diving and his parents kept screaming that he was their only hope. There was no improvement in sight, so, he got deeper into depression and started seeing his parents' love as highly conditional. Children who can't handle pressure will naturally think that committing suicide is the best option and a form of payback to their parents. Sadly, their last breaths will be the moment where they feel that they are in complete control of their lives.

Despite its widespread occurrence, suicide remains enveloped in stigma and misconceptions. The societal stigma surrounding suicide often prevents open conversations and discourages individuals from seeking timely help.

Robust research and data collection are foundational to understanding the trends and factors contributing to suicide. Insights driven by data can inform evidence-based policies and interventions, ultimately leading to more effective prevention efforts.

By acknowledging its global impact, unraveling the stigma, comprehending its complexity, and embracing a multidimensional approach, we take the initial step towards a safer and more compassionate world. After reading this book, you would have been equipped with knowledge, compassion, and actionable strategies to make a positive difference in the lives of those grappling with suicidal thoughts. Together, we all can work towards a future where hope prevails, and suicide is prevented.

The relationship between suicide and depression is one that goes beyond a simple correlation. In my case, they came intertwined to almost finish my destiny. My dad was a military man whose word was bond. He was an authoritarian who was more particular about finding survival means and economic empowerment. He had no cordial relationship with his wife or children. This eventually made my mom opt out of the marriage as she couldn't put up with the incessant fights, abuse and violence. Soon, my dad started having affairs with other women which made him entrust my care to them. He hardly spent time with me though he provided all my basic physical needs. I needed close friends and someone to confide in, so I fell into the wrong company in secondary school. I tried smoking and talking alcohol but the emotional emptiness lingered. I got involved in many atrocities because I wanted to belong to groups that could fill the void of love in my heart.

An incident that worsened my circumstance was a robbery that took place at our place and my parents valuables were carted away by the robbers. Being the black sheep of the family, I was the prime suspect. Every explanation I made in defense to my dad, fell on deaf ears. My family accused me of conniving with robbers, they tongue lashed me both in public and at home. The disgrace felt unbearable. My dad ordered an immediate arrest and I got locked up in a correctional centre for 7 days. Gradually, I became more entrenched in the knowledge of crimes through the tutelage of the criminals who had become my flat mates.

Thankfully, the real robbers got apprehended and confirmed that I had no hand in their act. Rather than apologise, my father maintained a straight face. According to him, I was up to no good and I was just a disaster about to happen. The few days I spent in prison seemed like years and I just felt there was nothing more to live for. If my own biological father could imagine that I connived with armed robbers to rob him, then I would never regain his trust, I thought. He had promised that he would stop at nothing to get me far away from his environment. I felt like a total failure as a first child; though I tried turning a new leaf, the constant discouragement from folks held me bound. Gradually, the thoughts of suicide crept in. In my innermost being, I was convinced that it was better to die than live with a stigma, so, I decided to drink a dangerous chemical substance known as snipper.

Numerous studies have shown that depression considerably increases the probability of suicidal thoughts, suicide attempts, and successful suicides. It's important to understand that not everyone who is depressed will attempt or really commit suicide, though. This risk can be reduced by a variety of protective factors, including social support, coping skills, and efficient treatment. On the other hand, the probability can rise in the presence of several aggravating variables such substance addiction, family history, and prior suicide attempts.

Let's examine some reasons why many people get depressed:

Childhood Trauma

The development of depression and other mental health disorders later in life is known to be significantly influenced by childhood trauma. The phrase "childhood trauma" serves as an umbrella word for a variety of traumatic events, including, but not limited to, physical and sexual abuse, emotional neglect, exposure to domestic violence, and parental separation or divorce. Such experiences can have a significant impact on mental health, frequently having long-lasting effects far into adulthood. For example, **physical abuse or bullying** on a child may make him develop a distorted sense of self-worth as well as persistent anxiety, both of which can result in depression. **Emotional neglect** is another type of trauma of children who do not receive enough emotional support from their parents or other caregivers. They may grow up feeling inadequate or unworthy, which increases their risk of developing depressive disorders later in life. Sexual abuse causes a major trauma for children and they frequently struggle with overwhelming shame and guilt, which can lead to depression in adolescence or adulthood. Similarly, children who experience **domestic violence between parents** frequently experience persistent anxiety and stress, which can lead to anxiety disorders and, later, despair.

These can cause a young person to feel unworthy and lead to the development of an uneasy attachment style that makes it difficult for the child to build trusting relationships with others.

Chronic Health Issues

A significant area of clinical interest and scientific attention is the connection between depressive disorders and chronic medical problems. Because of their protracted nature and negative effects on quality of life, chronic illnesses frequently serve as a breeding ground for psychological discomfort, such as depression. Consider the following important points: Stress on the Body: The body can be stressed physiologically by chronic disorders. Stress-related hormones like cortisol have the potential to influence neurotransmitters like serotonin, which may lead to the onset of depressive symptoms.

Reduced Quality of Life: Chronic illnesses limit one's ability to engage in physical exercise, engage in social relationships, or even pursue employment prospects. This results in a worse quality of life, which can trigger depressive episodes.

Depressive symptoms can be exacerbated by long-term medical conditions such diabetes, cardiovascular disease, and chronic pain syndromes. A person who has endured years of managing chronic pain may experience depression as a result of the ongoing psychological and physical toll.

Environmental Stressors

Many people have a strong emotional connection to environmental pressures on their mental health. At times, it seems as though the world is closing in on us and our anxieties and fears are weighing down even the air. It is incredibly painful for anyone who has experienced the crushing grip of despair brought on or made worse by outside factors. The following are some environmental stressors that takes emotional toll on us:

A new environment: Imagine yourself on the verge of a significant life transition, such as the start of a new career, a move across the country, or the termination of a committed relationship. The emotional turmoil is frequently severe. Your routine and comfort zone are abruptly disturbed, leaving you feeling vulnerable and lost. For some people, this is the start of a downward spiral towards depression.

Social Pressure: The implicit judgments, the continual focus on "what will people think," and the societal conventions can all contribute to a confining atmosphere. You continually compare yourself to what society expects of you, and when you feel unworthy, depression looks like an all-too-willing companion in your loneliness.

Stress at work: For people who toil in hazardous workplaces, every day is a challenge. There is a pit of melancholy feelings below, making you feel like you are walking a tightrope. Your feeling of wellbeing is corroded by the ongoing tension, and your self-esteem suffers blow after blow until you are physically and emotionally exhausted.

Financial Difficulties: Financial instability affects more than just the figures on a computer or the money on the table; it also causes constant anxiety. Depression is nourished by this ubiquitous stressor, which gives it the food it needs to develop into an all-consuming force inside of you.

Traumatic Events: People who have gone through trauma are aware of the severe emotional scars it leaves behind. The emotional impact of violent crimes, natural disasters, or the death of loved ones is profound. You're frequently left battling intrusive thoughts, worry, and a type of depression that seems to go on forever.

Chapter 2

—— THE WARNING SIGNS ——

epression, also known as major depressive disorder, is a common and serious mood disorder characterized by severe symptoms affecting a person's emotions, thoughts, and daily functioning. Diagnosis requires these symptoms to persist for at least 2 weeks. Different types of depression include:

Major depression: Persistent depressed mood or loss of interest for at least 2 weeks, significantly impacting daily life.
Persistent depressive disorder (dysthymia): Less severe symptoms lasting over 2 years.

Perinatal depression: Occurs during or after pregnancy, with prenatal and postpartum subtypes.

Seasonal affective disorder: Symptoms linked to seasonal changes, often in the winter.

Depression with psychosis: Severe form featuring delusions or hallucinations.

Bipolar disorder: Includes depressive and manic episodes, with elevated mood swings.

Depression can affect people of all ages, races, ethnicities, and genders. It can cause physical symptoms such as fatigue, changes in appetite, difficulty concentrating, and sleeping problems. It can also lead to feelings of hopelessness, low self-esteem, and difficulty making decisions. Treatment for depression usually involves a combination of medication, psychotherapy, and lifestyle changes.

Women are diagnosed with depression more often than men, but men can also be depressed. Depression can be caused by a variety of factors, including genetics, environment, and life events. Women may be more prone to depression due to certain hormones, such as estrogen and progesterone, as well as social and cultural factors. Men may be less likely to recognize, talk about, and seek help for their feelings or emotional problems, they are at greater risk of depression symptoms being undiagnosed or undertreated. This can be particularly dangerous for men, as depression can have serious health consequences if left untreated, such as an increased risk of heart disease, stroke, and suicide.

In order to prevent suicide, it is crucial to identify warning signs. Individuals who contemplate self-harm often exhibit observable signs of distress, signaling a need for support and assistance.

People who are considering suicide will often talk about it in a subtle way. They may crack jokes about it or sing it through songs and yet people around them may miss the gist. They may express feelings of hopelessness, talk about feeling trapped or being a burden to others, and even mention specific thoughts of self-harm. Once upon a time, a Nigerian rap artist released a single in his album where he sang that no one should cry at his demise. Surprisingly, in less than three months, the media reported his death.

It's very important to take words seriously and engage in open conversations with people who express their feelings in words as this can make a significant difference.

Similarly, changes in behaviour can indicate the emotional distress of an individual. If he/she withdraws from social interactions, loses interest in activities they once enjoyed, or exhibit recklessness or increases the use of substance, then these should not be ignored. Additionally, intense emotional swings, including extreme sadness, anger, anxiety, or irritability, may be indicative of underlying psychological struggles that people must pay attention to around them. When someone is exhibiting these traits or emotional shifts around you, you can offer support to prevent further distress.

Interestingly, physical changes, such as changes in sleep patterns, unexplained weight loss or gain, and fatigue, can accompany emotional distress. Individuals experiencing these physical symptoms may need professional help to address their underlying emotional struggles.

For someone going through depression, withdrawal and Isolation may be another warning sign to look out for. They have a tendency to withdraw from friends, family, and social activities. This isolation can worsen feelings of loneliness and hopelessness, making victims more susceptible to suicidal thoughts.

Also, in some cases, individuals contemplating suicide may give away their possessions or engage in behaviours that suggest they are preparing for their demise end. I once heard about a man who lost his wife to a terminal illness. His whole life had been centred around his wife within the last few years of her life. When she didn't make it, the man jokingly called on some of his friends and mentioned to them about his intention to sell his car and some other possessions. Initially, they waved it off but as he kept talking about it day in day out, one of them noticed an irrational tone in his voice over the phone and immediately visited him. It was at this point he noticed that his dear friend was battling depression as a result of his wife's death. He later opened up that he was losing his mind and didn't know what else to live for.

Although the experience of depression can vary in severity (e.g. from feeling irritable to feeling suicidal), you may notice the following common signs. You should be concerned if these signs persist over time, and affect the person's functioning.

- A depressed mood.
- Loss of enjoyment and interest in activities that used to be enjoyable.
- Lack of energy and tiredness.
- Feeling worthless or feeling guilty when they are not really at fault.
- Thinking about death a lot or of suicide.
- Difficulty concentrating or making decisions.
- Moving more slowly or sometimes becoming agitated and unable to settle.

- Having sleeping difficulties or sometimes sleeping too much.
- Loss of interest in food or sometimes eating too much.
- Changes in eating habits may lead to either loss of weight or putting on weight.

If you recognize any of these warning signs in someone you know, you should strike conversations or respond to them with compassion and empathy. Take their concerns seriously, listen actively, and encourage them to seek professional help. Each individual is different and not everyone who is experiencing depression will show the typical signs or symptoms of depression. Many people who experience depression may also be affected by other mental health problems like anxiety or substance use problems. However, do not assume that any signs or symptoms you have noticed means that the person is experiencing depression.

According to Mental Health First Aid Guidelines (2020), it's important to approach someone who may be experiencing depression with caution. Contrary to myth, talking about depression makes things better, not worse. If you think that someone you know may be depressed and needs help, first consider whether you are the best person to approach them or whether somebody else might be more appropriate. Ask the person if they are willing to talk to you, or if they would rather speak to someone else. If you are the best person or there is no one else, give the person opportunities to talk. Try to spend time with the person and gently bring up your concerns with them, e.g. mention that the person seems "not bright today". It can be helpful to let the person choose the moment to open up. However, if the person does not initiate a conversation with you about how they are feeling, you should say something to them. It is important to choose a suitable time when both you and the person are available to talk, as well as a private place where you both feel comfortable.

Let the person know that you are concerned about them and are willing to help. Ask the person if they would like to talk to you about how they are feeling. Focus on how the person is feeling and the changes you have noticed rather than the possibility that the person might have depression. If the person says that they are feeling sad or down, you should ask them how long they have been feeling that way and if they have spoken to anyone else about how they are feeling. Be prepared for the full range of reactions (e.g. relief, indifference, anger) when you approach the person. They may deny that they are experiencing changes in mood, behaviour or daily functioning. Remember, the person's thoughts, feelings and beliefs represent their own reality and you should be prepared to accept these without question. You should respect how the person interprets their symptoms. Some people who have recovered from depression may have a relapse of their symptoms. Don't assume that the person knows nothing about depression as they, or someone else close to them, may have experienced depression before.

However, even if the person has had a previous episode of depression, do not assume they will know how to manage the current episode. You should know sources of good quality information. If you give the person information, it is important that you give them resources that are accurate and appropriate to their situation, e.g. consider the person's literacy and ability to understand the information. Do not overwhelm the person with too much information or too many resources.

You may also check inward to ruminate on how you can offer support to depressed fellows. You must realise that recovering from depression solely lies on the individual. Treat him/her with respect and dignity, you should resist the urge to try to cure the person's depression or to come up with answers to their problems. Each person's situation and needs are unique. It is important to respect the person's autonomy while considering the extent to which they are able to make decisions for themselves, and whether they are at risk of harming themselves or others. Equally, you should respect the person's privacy unless you are concerned that the person is at risk of harming themselves or others. Offer consistent emotional support and understanding Although you may not be able to understand exactly how the person feels, let them know you care and want to help. Tell them that they are important to you, they are not alone and that you are there for them. It is more important for you to be genuinely caring than to say all the 'right things'. Let the person know that although their experience is very personal and painful, they are not alone. Often just taking the time to talk to or be with the person lets them know that someone cares.

The person needs additional support and understanding to help them through their illness, so you should be empathetic, compassionate and patient. It is important to be persistent and encouraging when supporting someone with depression. You should be consistent and predictable in your interactions with the person. People with depression are often overwhelmed by irrational fears and you need to be gentle and understanding of someone in this state. You should offer the person kindness and attention, even if it is not reciprocated. Your support is likely to be having a positive impact, even if it does not feel this way.

Encourage the person to talk to you. Encourage the person to talk about their thoughts, feelings, symptoms and any other problems they are experiencing. Explore with the person how their symptoms affect their daily life. Ask them if stress is a problem for them and, if it is, encourage them to find ways to reduce stress in their life. You can also ask whether something has happened to them recently that is contributing to how they are feeling. If the person does not want or have the energy to talk about how they are feeling, do not put pressure on them. Let them know that you are available to talk when they are ready. If the person finds it difficult to discuss their thoughts and feelings openly, suggest an activity that may make it easier for them to talk, e.g. have a cup of tea, go for a walk. You can also let the person know about available services where they can talk to someone else, e.g. a telephone counselling service. Be a good listener. You can help someone with depression by listening closely to them without expressing judgement. The key attitudes involved in non-judgmental listening are acceptance, genuineness and empathy. Adopt an attitude of acceptance of the person by withholding any and all judgments that you have made about the person or their circumstances. Set aside any negative beliefs and reactions in order to focus on the needs of the person you are helping and choose your words carefully so as to avoid causing offence, e.g. if you feel the person is being lazy, you should not express this. Rather, convey genuineness to the person by using body language that matches your verbal communication, e.g. telling the person you accept and respect their feelings, while maintaining an open posture and appropriate eye contact. Demonstrate empathy by showing the person that they are truly heard and understood, for example, say "What you are going through must be difficult."

Use the following non-verbal skills to reinforce non-judgmental communication:

Sit alongside the person and angled towards them, rather than directly opposite them. Notice how much personal space the person feels comfortable with and respect that.

Use the level of eye contact that the person seems most comfortable with. Maintain an open body position (e.g. not crossing arms, as this may appear defensive).

Avoid distracting gestures (e.g. fidgeting with a pen, glancing at other things or tapping your feet or fingers), as these could be interpreted as a lack of interest.

Be aware of the person's body language, as this can provide clues as to how they are feeling or how comfortable they are talking with you.

Be an active listener. Reflect back what the person has said to you before responding with your own thoughts. Do not interrupt the person when they are speaking, especially to share your own opinions or experiences. It is important to listen carefully to the person even if what they tell you is obviously not true or is misguided. Respect the person's feelings, personal values and experiences as valid, even if they are different from your own, or you disagree with them.

Other ways to be a good listener include:

Ask questions that show that you genuinely care and want to understand what they are saying. Ask open-ended questions to give the person an opportunity to say what they want to, e.g. "How are you feeling?" rather than "Are you feeling sad?".

Use minimal prompts when necessary to keep the conversation going, e.g. "I see" and "Mmmm".

Be okay with pauses and silences. While they may feel uncomfortable, the person may need time to think or find the right words.

Check your understanding by restating what the person has said and summarising facts and feelings.

Listen not only to what the person says, but how they say it, e.g. their tone of voice.

Use the same terminology that the person uses when discussing their experience, except if the person uses unhelpful or stigmatising language. If the person holds stigmatising attitudes towards mental illness, do your best to model acceptance. Have realistic expectations for the person You should accept the person as they are and have realistic expectations for them.

Everyday activities like cleaning the house, paying bills, or feeding the dog may seem overwhelming to the person. You should acknowledge that the person is not 'faking', 'lazy', 'weak' or 'selfish' and not push them to do activities that they feel are too much for them.

Acknowledge the person's strengths If the person judges themselves too harshly (e.g. saying that they are a weak person or a failure), remind them of their strengths and acknowledge any efforts they are making to get better. Let the person know that they are not weak or a failure because they have depression because strong and capable people can become depressed too. Tell them that you don't think less of them as a person. Give the person hope for recovery.

Encourage the person by telling them that, although they may not believe it now, with time and treatment, they will feel better. Offer hope of a more positive future in whatever form the person will accept and let them know that their life is important.

Depression is a medical illness and it is not the victim's fault that they are experiencing depression. It's not the best approach when you tell the person to "snap out of it", "get over it", "pull yourself together" or "get your acts together". If this was possible then the person would have done it. Do not tell the person "it is all in your head", or that they just need to stay busy or get out more. Do not trivialise the person's experiences by pressuring them to 'put a smile on their face', 'cheer up', or to 'lighten up'. Attempting to say something positive (e.g. "You don't seem that bad to me") can seem belittling or dismissive and should be avoided. Avoid applying any labels to the person that they may find stigmatising, e.g. 'mentally ill'. Also, do not use language related to a potential diagnosis when talking to the person, e.g. "It looks like you have major depressive disorder".

Avoid speaking to the person with an over-involved or over-protective attitude. Do not nag the person to try to get them to do what they normally would and avoid confrontation, unless necessary to prevent the person from carrying out harmful or dangerous acts. Do not suggest the use of alcohol or other drugs to feel better.

If the person is not communicating well (e.g. speaking slower, less clear than usual or being repetitive), be patient and accept these responses as the best the person has to offer at the moment. Try to be as supportive as possible. Do not interrupt, criticise, express frustration or be hostile or sarcastic. Try to see any irritable or unpleasant behaviours as part of the illness and not take these personally. If the person becomes angry during the conversation, do not make assumptions about the cause of their anger. Try to stay calm and acknowledge the person's anger. However, do not accept abuse or compromise your own mental health when helping the person. If the person doesn't feel comfortable talking to you, encourage them to discuss how they are feeling with someone else. If cultural differences are interfering with your ability to help the person, you should discuss with the person what is culturally appropriate and realistic for them. Be willing to adjust your verbal and non-verbal behaviours, e.g. the person may be comfortable with a different level of eye contact or may be used to more personal space. You can also talk to a mental health service that specialises in working with people from different cultural backgrounds, if available. Helping someone who is depressed may evoke an unexpected emotional response in you.

SEEK PROFESSIONAL HELP

It is important that you recognise when to encourage the depressed person to seek professional help especially when depression lasts for weeks and affects a person's functioning in daily life. Interestingly, a person's depression will not just go away at the inception of therapy, though early treatment brings the best outcomes. It is also important that you do not lie or make excuses for the person's behaviour, as this may delay getting assistance. Seek immediate professional help if the person is experiencing hallucinations or delusions. You should have some general knowledge about the types of treatment that can be helpful for depression. You should also know about what services are available in the person's local area and the local pathways to professional help, e.g. referral from a General Practitioner in order to see a specialist. These may vary depending on the person's cultural background or religious beliefs. Meanwhile, discuss the benefits of seeking professional help and ask the person whether they think it would benefit them. Talk about professional help seeking as a natural action to take, explain that mental health problems are common and treatable.

Depression is often not recognised by health professionals and it may take some time to get a diagnosis and find a healthcare provider with whom the person is able to establish a good relationship. Encourage the person not to give up seeking appropriate professional help. If the person's behaviour is having a negative effect on you, recognise your own feelings.
If the person is at risk of harming themselves or others, you should consider the safety of all involved, and take any necessary protective action, e.g. call an ambulance, emergency services, or mental health crisis team. Ask the person to take steps to get help.

Recognizing warning signs and understanding the signals of distress can empower individuals and communities to intervene early and prevent suicide. By being vigilant, compassionate, and proactive, we can create a supportive environment where those struggling with suicidal thoughts find the help and understanding they need to overcome their pain. Together, we can make a difference in the lives of those at risk and work towards a future where suicide is averted, and hope and resilience prevail.

Chapter 3

SUICIDE IN THE SOCIETY

Loneliness and Isolation

Human beings are social creatures, and our relationships with others profoundly influence our well-being. Social factors, such as the quality of our connections and the support we receive, play a crucial role in suicide risk. Loneliness is an epidemic that affects people of all ages and backgrounds. It can stem from a variety of factors, including social isolation, lack of close relationships, and feelings of alienation. Individuals experiencing loneliness may feel disconnected from others, leading to a sense of hopelessness and vulnerability.

Social isolation is a condition where individuals have limited or no social interactions or engagement with others. This state of disconnection can be both a cause and consequence of loneliness. For some, social isolation is a result of mental health challenges or life circumstances, while for others, it may lead to a deterioration of mental health.

Loneliness and social isolation can have a significant impact on mental health, contributing to depression, anxiety, and other psychological disorders.

Certain groups are more vulnerable to loneliness and social isolation. These include the elderly, individuals living in rural areas, people with disabilities, and those who identify as LGBTQ+. Understanding the unique challenges faced by these populations is crucial in designing targeted interventions.

Creating supportive communities is a key strategy in preventing suicide. Fostering a sense of belonging and connectedness can act as a protective factor against suicide risk. Community organizations, schools, workplaces, and other institutions can play a pivotal role in providing social support.

Nurturing Resilience in Vulnerable Youths

Suicide among the youths is a deep and complex issue. Adolescence is a time of significant physical, emotional, and social changes, making young people particularly vulnerable to mental health challenges.

Adolescence is marked by the search for identity, peer pressure, academic stress, and family dynamics. For some youth, these challenges can become overwhelming, leading to feelings of hopelessness and despair. Additionally, experiences of bullying, discrimination, or trauma can further increase the risk of suicidal thoughts.

Behaviour is always a communication, even though we may not always realise it. Imagine a really bad day, you go home and within minutes you find yourself arguing with someone in your family. You probably didn't plan to take out your frustration on those closest to you, but that's what happened. Many vulnerable youths are likely to have had times when they haven't felt safe and they end up reacting to all sorts of triggers in order to keep themselves safe or feel safe (which of course may be very different things). Similarly, they've often experienced multiple rejections. Many will have accompanying attachment issues and sometimes will "reject" before they can be rejected. They may push you away because this may be less painful than allowing you to reject them. Or it may be that certain behaviours give them access to a person they are developing an attachment to, so their message is "I need that person". By acknowledging this, and recognising that what a student needs more than anything is to build relationships that help them feel safe, we may be able to adjust our reactions appropriately.

The rise of social media has brought both benefits and challenges to youth mental health. While social media provides a platform for connection and self-expression, it can also expose young people to cyberbullying, unrealistic comparisons, and a constant pressure to fit in. Understanding the impact of social media on youth mental health is crucial in promoting healthy online behaviours. Teenagers are having a harder time imagining their lives without social media. Practitioners must be able to evaluate risk, and social media may be a novel factor to take into account. The notion of the connection between social media and mental health is strongly impacted by teenage and professional opinions, despite the fact that there is little actual data to back up the allegation. Risks linked with this population's use of social media include privacy issues, cyberbullying, detrimental effects on education and mental health, among others. However, responsible social media use can increase the chances of meeting others and having a conversation while also improving one's health, self-esteem, and access to vital medical information.

Stigma surrounding mental health is particularly prevalent among young people. Fear of judgment and rejection may prevent youth from seeking help for their emotional struggles, so they may resort to becoming lone rangers who prefer to be alone most of the time.

In recent years, an alarming rise in loneliness among young people has emerged in the realm of mental health. A study published in July 2021 revealed that adolescents today are experiencing loneliness at twice the rate they did a decade ago. These findings bring to light the surprising reality that, despite being the most technologically connected generation, young people are paradoxically more vulnerable to loneliness. Even in the digital age, young people seem to be struggling with loneliness more than any other age group.

The rise in loneliness appears to be linked with the increased availability of smartphones and internet use. As the study suggests, the psychological well-being of adolescents started declining around 2012, coinciding with the widespread adoption of smartphones and increased internet usage. Paradoxically, the very technology designed to connect people may be contributing to feelings of isolation.

For example, adolescents who haven't had the time to develop effective coping strategies for dealing with loneliness, can become confused about their feelings especially when they see social media showcasing the "perfect" lives of other people. They can begin to feel pained because of the fear of missing out on experiences. At this age when they are even in the process of forming their identity, feelings of isolation may come up once in a while.

The impact of loneliness on youths is so profound that it has serious consequences for both mental and physical health. It is strongly linked to depression, substance abuse, and a higher risk of suicide among isolated youths. Some isolated and depressed youths smoke at least 15 cigarettes a day which is detrimental to their health, raises their stress levels, leads to inflammation, and increases the risk of heart disease, arthritis and diabetes. Thankfully, I didn't contact any of these diseases while frolicking in my youthful exuberance because God decided to have mercy on me. Some youths have contacted serious terminal diseases through this wasted lifestyle.

Meanwhile, we can reduce loneliness among the youths by having meaningful face-to-face interactions with them where they feel free to unbundle their heart concerning many issues. Young people need to be in spaces where they can spend time with family who will give them a sense of belonging and offer companionship when needed. This will even encourage them to get around eight hours of sleep daily because after having series of activities with family and friends, the body will naturally demand for adequate rest.

Young people who are prone to depression can become better when they participate in regular exercises and physical activities. Also, reducing the time spent on platforms like Facebook, Instagram, and Snapchat has been shown to reduce feelings of loneliness and depression too.

Loneliness among young people is a growing concern with profound implications for their mental and physical health. Recognizing the factors contributing to this issue and implementing strategies to mitigate its impact are essential steps toward fostering a healthier, more connected generation. Building healthy habits, promoting meaningful in-person interactions, and educating young people about emotional well-being can go a long way in combating the loneliness epidemic among today's youth. Together, we can work towards a society where youth feel valued, understood, and empowered, making mental well-being a top priority.

Understanding and Providing Support for the Elderly

Loneliness is an emotional state of mind wherein a person feels alone. This feeling may arise whether the person is alone or surrounded by people. Old people feel lonely not only because there are less people around them or they explore less but also because nobody understands their emotion. An elderly woman was angry that the disparity between her days as a youth and her days in old age is too overwhelming. She had some identity and people listened to her but now, no one wants to talk to her and this is fast eating her up.

Loneliness can happen when a person does not enjoy his own company. He believes that happiness lies only in the company of others. In fact, some people have low self-esteem, so they do not feel connected with others. They have a strong feeling that they are not liked by people and that they are a burden to others. On the other hand, people who have good relations with people usually do not feel lonely. If while in their youth, they spent time listening to others and helping others, they may not likely be lonely in their old age. So, the person who does not maintain good relationship with people, suffers later.

For a young professional who has worked in different jobs, old age will take its toll after retirement. He just realizes that he can't run around as before and may feel useless if he has nothing doing. However, after getting retirement, some personal works should keep him active such as being a consultant in the field of his specialization. This would bring him in contact with youngsters who need counsel or mentorship along their career path.

Likewise, the work can be social service, some kind of teaching or delivering lectures at conferences. If your presence is helpful for people in anyway, you will be wanted everywhere. Try to explore new options and this will help you feel worthy and confident.

Loneliness is a prevalent issue among the elderly, especially for those who are not outspoken or friendly and those may have lost their spouses, friends, or family members. Social isolation can further worsen these feelings leading to a sense of disconnectedness and increasing the risk of depression and suicidal thoughts.

The aging process often comes with health challenges, chronic conditions, and limitations in mobility. Coping with these changes can be emotionally taxing, especially if individuals feel burdensome or dependent on others. Addressing both physical and mental health needs is crucial. As one grows older, the experience of loss becomes more common. Grief over the loss of loved ones, loss of independence, or the end of a fulfilling career can be overwhelming. Providing bereavement support and validating these feelings is essential for emotional well-being.

It is even important to employ caregivers who will provide succour to elderly people especially those with chronic illnesses or disabilities. Fostering social connections is vital in preventing suicide among the elderly. Community programs, senior centers, and support groups can offer opportunities for socialization and reduce feelings of isolation.

It's also important to encourage open conversations about mental health with elderly people so as to break the stigma and create a supportive environment to share their feelings and concerns. An elderly friend was invited to speak at an elders' summit to rub minds with them. One of the things he emphasized on was the difference between loneliness and solitude. According to him. loneliness reveals inside the pain of being alone, while solitude takes joy in spending time with yourself. Loneliness is a pity party feeding the ego, while solitude is a celebration of yourself, by yourself, feeding the soul.

Loneliness may bring feelings of incompleteness while solitude makes you discover the beauty of your gifts as God's creation. He reveals different things to you that you may not have thought about yourself and you just want to grow that relationship more with him. You are so much more than you know, so much more beautiful and perfect than you've ever dreamed yourself to be. When you discover in you the gifts of God, loneliness will give way to solitude.

God wants you to be a light to other people so that when your family members are far away, He will bring other young people around you to give you support and keep you company. You could attend events, read books to remain mentally active. Don't hold yourself aloof; never become judgmental as you will be disliked by others; learn new things especially how to surf the internet because this can bring a lot of engagements and discoveries too.

Suicide among the elderly is a complex and preventable issue. By understanding the unique challenges faced by this population and providing support, compassion, and mental health care, we can create a society where older adults feel valued, connected, and respected. Through a collective effort, we can protect our elderly population from the devastating impact of suicide and ensure that they experience their later years with dignity, support, and emotional well-being. On a lighter note, young people need to spend time with their grandparents or aged people so as to tap from their wealth of experience and knowledge. Even when they are wrong on some issues, don't argue with them for their mental health sake. Just relish the moment of your togetherness.

Embracing Inclusivity in the LGBTQ+ Community

The concept of intersectionality acknowledges that people have numerous facets of identity that interact and overlap, influencing their experiences and oppressive systems. It is critical to recognize the special difficulties experienced by those who navigate overlapping identities, such as race, ethnicity, gender, and disability, in the context of LGBTQ+ activism. We can better comprehend the LGBTQ+ community and make sure that no one is left out by embracing intersectionality. It is crucial to put those with marginalized identities at the core of the LGBTQ+ movement in order to make it truly inclusive. In order to do this, we must actively seek out and magnify the perspectives of people who experience various forms of discrimination. By doing this, we recognize the various battles that exist within the community and further the goal of destroying overlapping oppressive institutions.

LGBTQ+ activism that takes an intersectional approach challenges presumptions and prejudices that support inequality and exclusion. By acknowledging the distinctive experiences of LGBTQ+ people with marginalized identities, we can refute the idea that the LGBTQ+ community is homogeneous. This enables us to address the particular needs and issues of many groups within the larger movement, promoting a more inclusive and equitable environment.

Intersectional LGBTQ+ action is based on cooperation and solidarity. By building environments that foster communication, mutual learning, and collaboration amongst people with various identities and experiences, we can swiftly break down barriers and create bridges.

The LGBTQ+ population experiences certain difficulties that may raise the risk of suicide. Feelings of rejection and isolation can result from bias, discrimination, and social stigma. In order to offer assistance and encourage suicide prevention, it is essential to understand the particular problems faced by LGBTQ+ people. Despite the fact that there may not be a majority of LGBTQ+ people, it is important to acknowledge that their experiences are important and real. People can change their perspective from focusing on their minority status to embracing the strength and resilience that come from their unique experiences by acknowledging and enjoying the diversity within the LGBTQ+ community. A more inclusive society can only be created with the help of education, open-mindedness, and empathy.

One of the best strategies to deal with emotions of loneliness or self-doubt is self-acceptance which is a critical aspect of personal growth and emotional well-being. For LGBTQ+ individuals, embracing their identity and experiences can help them overcome feelings of guilt or self-blame. Personal empowerment can be achieved by focusing on self-love, self-compassion, and taking ownership of one's unique journey.

If feelings of self-blame or guilt persist, seeking professional help can be a valuable resource. Therapists and counselors experienced in LGBTQ+ issues can provide a safe space for individuals to explore their emotions and work towards self-acceptance. Mental health professionals can equip individuals with coping strategies and tools to navigate the emotional complexities that may arise from their unique experiences.

The emotional journey of LGBTQ+ individuals is a complex and deeply personal process. It's essential to acknowledge and validate their experiences, both during moments of pleasure and in times of solitude. By embracing self-acceptance, building supportive networks, and fostering a more inclusive society, LGBTQ+ individuals can thrive and enjoy their lives to the fullest, without the burden of self-blame or doubt.

Suicide prevention in the LGBTQ+ community requires understanding the challenges faced by individuals due to discrimination, stigma, and rejection. By promoting inclusivity, providing mental health support, and fostering understanding and acceptance, we can create a world where LGBTQ+ individuals feel valued, safe, and empowered to live their lives authentically. Together, we can work towards a future where suicide is no longer a heartbreaking reality for the LGBTQ+ community.

Coping with Trauma and Stress in the Armed Forces

Military service can expose individuals to significant levels of trauma, stress, and hardship. Serving in the armed forces often involves exposure to life-threatening situations, witnessing violence, and experiencing the emotional toll of combat. Understanding the unique challenges faced by service members is crucial in addressing the issue of suicide in the armed forces.

One of the most prominent issues associated with military service is PTSD- (Post-Traumatic Stress Disorder). It is a common mental health condition among military personnel, resulting from exposure to traumatic events. The symptoms of PTSD, such as intrusive memories, flashbacks, and emotional numbness, can significantly impact a service member's well-being and increase their risk of suicide. The human mind is incomprehensible. We all perceive the world differently, even in the middle of a fight. The mind of a soldier in a combat is like a battlefield that is centred on survival strategy only. It's either he wins or loses!

Combat is a major stressor to the brain and human psyche that makes the entire body of a soldier go into survival mode with adrenaline pumping and mind going 100 miles an hour. The body is geared up to fight or flight and within minutes, it's all over. What seemed like 5 hours was only 10 minutes and this leaves him exhausted and his hands shaking. The adrenaline in the body fades and the world slows back down. Then the soldier takes account of himself and others and sees that he is alive.

There's a lot of stress for the human brain and human psyche to endure. Many times, combat replays over and over in the head of the soldier. He perceives the world differently and his brain becomes unsettled.

Having a family member in the military opened me up to experiences that makes me wonder why such profession exists. He goes on peace-keeping missions, fights in war zones and comes back home to deal with sleepless nights and a disturbed mind. Definitely, military people handle the trauma of combat differently.

In the military culture, seeking help for mental health issues is often stigmatized. Fear of judgment, concerns about career advancement, and a sense of duty can prevent service members from seeking the support they need. For most of them who retire, transitioning from military to civilian life can be challenging. Veterans may struggle to readjust to civilian society, face unemployment, or experience a loss of purpose. Adequate support and resources are essential during this transitional period to reduce suicide risk.

Sometimes, many of them resort to substance abuse as a coping mechanism to deal with trauma and stress. Unfortunately, it can lead to a vicious cycle of addiction and aggravate the feeling of hopelessness, increasing suicide risk. Traumatic experiences can leave deep emotional scars, potentially increasing an individual's vulnerability to suicidal thoughts. This requires specialized treatment to address the underlying pain and prevent suicidal tendencies.

Creating a culture that encourages seeking mental health support is vital in suicide prevention within the military. Offering confidential and accessible mental health services can help service members cope with the emotional toll of their experiences. They need trauma-informed care which recognizes the impact of trauma on mental health and tailors treatment accordingly. Implementing trauma-informed approaches in mental health care for service members can lead to more effective interventions.

Similarly, peer support and the camaraderie among service members can be a valuable protective factor against suicide. Encouraging open conversations and offering support within the military community can foster a sense of belonging and understanding. More so, it's important to identify high-risk individuals in suicide prevention. Regular mental health screenings, early intervention, and monitoring for warning signs can save lives. Collaborations between the military, veterans' organizations, and mental health professionals will go a long way to prevent suicide among military personnel.

Suicide prevention in the armed forces requires a multifaceted approach that addresses the mental health challenges and stressors faced by service members. By promoting mental health support, reducing stigma, and creating an environment that fosters resilience and camaraderie, we can honour the sacrifice of those who serve by ensuring their well-being and preventing suicide within the military community. Together, we can work towards a future where military personnel receive the support they need to navigate the emotional complexities of their service and transition to civilian life successfully.

Creating an environment where mental health is openly discussed and accepted can reduce the shame associated with seeking help. Encouraging empathy and understanding can make individuals feel more comfortable reaching out for support.

In the digital age, technology can both facilitate and hinder social connections. While social media platforms allow individuals to connect globally, they can also contribute to feelings of loneliness and isolation. Promoting positive online interactions and using technology to build meaningful relationships can be beneficial.

Support networks and peer support programs can provide a lifeline to individuals experiencing loneliness. Connecting individuals with similar experiences can create a sense of belonging and offer validation, fostering emotional well-being.

Educating communities about the importance of social connections and the impact of loneliness can lead to collective efforts in supporting those at risk. Community outreach programs can identify and reach individuals who may be experiencing social isolation and provide necessary resources.

Understanding the influence of social factors, loneliness, and isolation on suicide risk is essential in developing comprehensive suicide prevention strategies. By prioritizing social connections, creating supportive communities, and reducing stigma, we can cultivate an environment where individuals feel valued, connected, and supported. Together, we can build a society where no one feels alone, and the journey towards suicide prevention is guided by empathy, compassion, and solidarity.

Chapter 4

UNRAVELING THE COMPLEXITIES OF SUICIDE

Suicide is an outcome of deep psychological distress and pain. There is a long-term struggle on the part of these people, as well as traumatizing experiences and sorrow among their family and friends, behind every suicide attempt and attempt at suicide. Together, it is clear that preventing suicide is a top issue on a global scale. To improve the detection, intervention, and ultimately the prevention of suicide and suicidal behaviour, clinicians and researchers must make every effort to improve suicide prevention. The primary goal is to advance interdisciplinary knowledge of the causes, contributing factors, and facilitators of suicidality.

Suicide is a very intricate and nuanced phenomena, with numerous enabling and supporting factors. The combination of a number of variables, including neurobiology, personal and family history, stressful events, and sociocultural environment, may determine it. Given that it's one of the most severe human behaviours, a distinct focus would be to identify the underlying psychological processes that may lead to suicidal ideation and behaviour.

To comprehend the intricate nature of suicide, we must delve into the psychological factors that contribute to such drastic decisions such as exploring the complexities of the human mind and the psychological base of suicide.

Mental health disorders, such as depression, bipolar disorder, schizophrenia, and anxiety, are closely linked to suicidal ideation. Individuals grappling with these conditions may experience overwhelming despair and hopelessness, leading them to consider suicide as a way to escape their emotional pain. People generally think that people who commit suicide are cowards or they are just weak people who can't handle their challenges. Very few people actually understand what a person goes through to have reached this decision.

Taking one's life is an action that culminates from a series of events in one's life. For instance, think of yourself in a really dark path at night unable to see the right way even if you can hear your friends and family trying to guide you, but you are unable to hear or understand them. So, the only thing that stays in your mind is that you are all alone and you just want to end this struggle. This is exactly what depression does to people, it makes people deaf towards any kind of external help. However, many people back out just before they are about to do it, they get to hear the long-lost voices echoing at the back of their mind. They come out and start asking for help. When they get it, they become stronger than ever before.

This was my experience after I had battled suicidal thoughts in my head and mind. I wanted to stop being a menace to my family but the more I fought so hard, the harder I got in the mess. I had wanted to end it all together because no one cared about me, they left me in my dark thoughts but just at the point of anxiety and utter feeling of hopelessness, a light shone on my path. Thankfully, God brought a young woman my way who started counselling and encouraging me. She made me see beyond my flaws and I began to realise how much God loved me.

Emotions are an integral part of the human experience, and extreme emotional distress can drive individuals to contemplate suicide. Feelings of isolation, shame, guilt, and worthlessness can become unbearable burdens, pushing individuals towards self-destructive thoughts. While depression is seemingly more common and suicide is one of the leading causes of death worldwide, the average person is NOT suicidal. Many equate it to being simply 'depressed', or just being 'sad' for a period of time.

Many people do not know that suicidal thoughts, most times, come as a result of underlying severe mental problems that haven't been addressed. It is not even remotely comparable to just feeling 'depressed'. It also unfortunately isn't something that ever truly goes away for some people. Some try to cope with it, while others succumb to it.

It's also an anomaly to assume that the rich, successful and powerful people don't have suicidal thoughts but that's not true. People equate someone's success and what they have in their bank account to mean they are automatically happy and should be happy. However, feeling suicidal doesn't discriminate, and can impact anybody regardless of social class. Suicide is a big cancer and barrier that one needs a higher support to overcome or break through.

Compassionate emotional support and psychological therapy can offer a lifeline to those feeling overwhelmed by their emotions. Negative cognitive patterns, such as persistent negative thoughts and distorted perceptions, can contribute to the development of suicidal thoughts. Cognitive Behavioral Therapy (CBT) and other therapeutic approaches can help individuals recognize and challenge these patterns, fostering a more positive outlook on life.

Hope and despair are powerful emotions that sway an individual's decision-making process. Losing hope can lead to a sense of resignation and a belief that nothing will ever improve. Conversely, fostering hope can offer a lifeline to those on the brink, reminding them that there are better days ahead. Encouraging hope and resilience through therapy and support can be life-saving. When faced with overwhelming emotional pain, individuals may resort to maladaptive coping mechanisms, such as substance abuse or self-harm. These behaviours provide temporary relief but have long lasting side effects in the long run. Understanding healthier coping strategies and providing alternative outlets for emotional expression is vital.

Similarly, social and cultural factors also shape an individual's perception of suicide and influence their coping strategies. Societies that stigmatize mental health or glorify suicide can create additional barriers for those seeking help. Embracing a culture of empathy, open communication, and mental health awareness is crucial in breaking down these barriers.

Recognizing and interpreting suicidal communication is essential for intervention. Sometimes, individuals may indirectly express their distress through verbal cues, artwork, or social media posts. In fact, many young persons are more expressive through their social media posts. They may joke about suicide and depression but it's expedient to pay attention to these subtle signals because Nigerians say "we get to know the truth from play."

Understanding the psychology of suicide provides us with essential insights into the web of emotions, thoughts, and experiences that lead individuals to contemplate taking their own lives. By recognizing the interplay of mental health, emotions, cognitive patterns, trauma, coping mechanisms, and societal influences, we gain the knowledge necessary to respond with empathy, compassion, and effective interventions. In the journey towards suicide prevention, empathy and understanding form the bedrock upon which hope and healing can thrive.

Chapter 5

MENTAL HEALTH
AND UNDERLYING
CONDITIONS

Mental health plays a pivotal role in suicide risk and prevention. Understanding and addressing underlying mental health conditions is crucial in providing effective support to individuals at risk. This chapter delves into the intricate relationship between mental health and suicide, highlighting the importance of mental health care in suicide prevention.

One significant barrier to mental health care is the persistent stigma surrounding mental illnesses. Stigmatizing attitudes may prevent individuals from seeking help, fearing judgment and discrimination. By fostering open conversations about mental health and promoting empathy, we can work towards eradicating the stigma and encouraging individuals to seek the support they need.

If you are concerned the person may be at risk of suicide, you need to approach them and have a conversation about your concerns. In preparing yourself to approach the person, you have to be aware of your own attitudes about suicide and the impact of these on your ability to provide assistance (e.g. beliefs that suicide is wrong or that it is a rational option). If the person is from a different cultural or religious background to your own, keep in mind that they might have beliefs and attitudes about suicide which differ from your own. Be aware that it is more important to genuinely want to help than to be of the same age, gender or cultural background as the person. If you feel unable to ask the person about suicidal thoughts, find someone else who can.

Making the approach Act promptly if you think someone is considering suicide. Even if you only have a mild suspicion that the person is having suicidal thoughts, you should still approach them. Tell the person you care and want to help. Tell them your concerns about them, describing behaviours that have caused you to be concerned about suicide. However, understand that the person may not want to talk with you. If you are unable to make a connection with the person, help them to find someone else to talk to.

You may feel like asking anyone who could have thoughts of suicide but don't ask about suicide in leading or judgmental ways (e.g. 'You're not thinking of doing anything stupid, are you?'). Sometimes people are reluctant to ask directly about suicide because they think they will put the idea in the person's head. This is not true. Similarly, if a person is suicidal, asking them about suicidal thoughts will not increase the risk that they will act on it. Instead, asking the person about suicidal thoughts will allow them the chance to talk about their problems and show them that somebody cares.

Although it is common to feel panic or shock when someone discloses thoughts of suicide, it is important to avoid expressing negative reactions. Do your best to appear calm, confident and empathic in the face of the suicide crisis, as this may have a reassuring effect for the suicidal person. It is more important to be genuinely caring than to say 'all the right things'. Be supportive and understanding of the suicidal person, and listen to them with undivided attention.

Suicidal thoughts are often a plea for help and a desperate attempt to escape from problems and distressing feelings. Ask the suicidal person what they are thinking and feeling. Reassure them that you want to hear whatever they have to say. Allow them to talk about these thoughts and feelings, and their reasons for wanting to die and acknowledge these. Let the suicidal person know it is okay to talk about things that might be painful, even if it is hard. Allow them to express their feelings (e.g. allow them to cry, express anger, or scream). A suicidal person may feel relief at being able to do so. Remember to thank the suicidal person for sharing their feelings with you and acknowledge the courage this takes.

Listening tips

● Be patient and calm while the suicidal person is talking about their feelings.

● Listen to the suicidal person without expressing judgment, accepting what they are saying without agreeing or disagreeing with their behaviour or point of view.

● Ask open-ended questions (i.e. questions that cannot be simply answered with 'yes' or 'no') to find out more about the suicidal thoughts and feelings and the problems behind these.

● Show you are listening by summarising what the suicidal person is saying.

● Clarify important points with the person to make sure they are fully understood.

● Express empathy for the suicidal person.

What not to do
Don't...
● ... argue or debate with the person about their thoughts of suicide.

● ... discuss with the person whether suicide is right or wrong.

● ... use guilt or threats to prevent suicide (e.g. do not tell the person they will go to hell or ruin other people's lives if they die by suicide).

● ... minimise the suicidal person's problems.

● ... give glib 'reassurance' such as "don't worry", "cheer up", "you have everything going for you" or "everything will be alright".

● ... interrupt with stories of your own.

● ... communicate a lack of interest or negative attitude through your body language.

● ... 'call their bluff' (dare or tell the suicidal person to 'just do it').

● ... attempt to give the suicidal person a diagnosis of a mental illness. Do not avoid using the word 'suicide'.

It is important to discuss the issue directly without dread or expressing negative judgement. Demonstrate appropriate language when referring to suicide by using the terms 'suicide' or 'die by suicide', and avoiding the use of terms to describe suicide that promote stigmatising attitudes, e.g. 'commit suicide' (implying it is a crime or sin) or referring to past suicide attempts as having 'failed' or been 'unsuccessful', implying death would have been a favourable outcome.

Depression: A Major Contributor

Depression is one of the most common mental health conditions associated with suicide. Its hallmark symptoms of persistent sadness, loss of interest, and feelings of worthlessness can overwhelm individuals, leading them to contemplate suicide as a means of escape. Early detection and evidence-based treatments, such as psychotherapy and antidepressant medication, can be effective in alleviating depression and reducing suicide risk.

Here are some practical strategies for helping others who are facing depression. However, never assume there are no medical issues that need attention.

Describe the experience. Ask people to describe their experience of depression in vivid detail. People are different, so depression comes in many shapes and sizes.

Identify the causes. Depression often is not just something we have, it is something we do. Invite people to examine their own hearts with this question: If your depression could speak, what would it say? What does it say about you? To others? To God? Depression is an active experience and can result from many sources other than the physiological guilt due to unconfessed sin, false guilt, misplaced shame, ungodly fears, suppressed bitterness or hatred, hopeless grieving, and unbiblical expectations.

Read and observe Scripture. Ask people with whom you work to study Psalms 42-43. How does the psalmist address God? What does he preach to himself?

Act on the truth. Those who seek help first must accept the challenge of faithful obedience, even though they do not feel like it and are skeptical that anything will make a difference, it's important to have faith. Also, explain to them that progress out of the pit is step-by-step, bit-by-bit. Small, practical, consistent faith-based change occurs in the details.

Look at lifestyle. Evaluate and provide recommendations for lifestyle problems, such as overworking, lack of exercise, sleep difficulties, procrastination, unresolved stressors, absence of spiritual disciplines. Resolve conflicts. Deal with troubled relationships, past or present.

Get to work. Assign active loving tasks performed for the benefit of others. Helping others can provide a new perspective on life.

See a doctor. Refer depressed persons to a Christian physician to rule out physical causes if a physician has not been contacted already. Persons who are already taking multiple medications may need a physician's care to avoid further complications.

Encouraging individuals to seek help from mental health professionals is crucial in addressing underlying mental health conditions. Providing accessible and affordable mental health services can ensure that individuals receive the care they need to manage their mental health effectively. Family and friends play a vital role in supporting individuals with mental health challenges. Offering non-judgmental emotional support, actively listening, and encouraging their loved ones to seek professional help can be instrumental in their journey towards recovery.

Addressing underlying mental health conditions is fundamental to suicide prevention. By prioritizing mental health care, reducing stigma, and offering comprehensive support, we can create a world where individuals feel empowered to seek help and receive the care they need. Together, we can break down barriers to mental health treatment, promoting emotional well-being, and reducing the devastating impact of suicide on individuals and communities.

As far as I'm concerned, depression is not simply a medical problem or a mental problem, it's more like human problem. While medical and emotional problems can and often do contribute to depression, for others, this illness has very significant spiritual components.

The holy book in Proverbs 12:25 mentions depression directly, "Anxiety in the heart of man causes depression, but a good word makes it glad" (NKJV). In this little couplet God, via the wisdom of king Solomon, provides both a diagnosis and prescription that can help people grow beyond depression. A heart full of anxiety is the culprit. Jesus said:

"Come to Me, all you who are weary and burdened, and I will give you rest. Take My yoke upon you, and learn from Me, because I am gentle and humble in heart, and you will find rest for your souls. For My yoke is easy, and My burden is light".

Matthew 11:28-30

Hopelessness is one of the hallmark symptoms of depression and one Bible character whose adulthood was punctuated by it, alongside sorrows and tribulation was Paul. In spite of his suffering, He said "We have placed our hope in Him that He will deliver us again"(2 Corinthians 1:10b). No one can truly overcome depression without God. On a daily basis, He encourages us to call on Him in the day of trouble and He will deliver us.

We live in a fallen world, one in which good things may come to an end. The tragic dimension of life will be present until the kingdom of God comes fully in the second coming of Christ. The joy of salvation comes from realizing, again and again, that our sins have been forgiven and that we will live forever with God, who desires that we share in His joy in eternity.

I surrendered my life to Christ after all efforts proved abortive. I thought I could outsmart my depression. In fact, at a point, I crossed the line with the lady who became a counsellor to me and offered me her shoulder to lean on. She got pregnant for me and my family started another war with me. This further drove me down the suicide lane but one day, my dad saw an opportunity for me to travel abroad. He refused my marriage to the girl and instructed my immediate exit from Nigeria but I was determined not to reject my unborn child like I was rejected so I did a secret court wedding with the lady before leaving.

I kept in touch with her and somewhere along the line, someone preached about God's love to me that captivated my heart. I decided to reciprocate by loving God with all my heart, soul, mind and strength.

Chapter 6

MEDIA AWARENESS AND CYBERBULLYING

In the digital age, technology has become an integral part of our lives, influencing how we communicate, connect, and access information. While technology offers numerous benefits, it also poses challenges to mental health and suicide prevention. On one hand, responsible reporting can help raise awareness and reduce stigma.

One of the major issues in the media is cyberbullying which seriously affecting not just the young victims, but also the victims' families, the bully, and those who witness instances of cyberbullying. However, the effect of cyberbullying can be most detrimental to the victim, of course, as they may experience a number of emotional issues that affect their social and academic performance as well as their overall mental health.

As parents today, you may not have ever experienced cyberbullying yourself. It may be hard to fathom how some words of text on a computer screen can lead to such trauma. After all, bullying has seemingly always been a facet of school and on the playground. Perhaps you have seen or experienced bullying when you were in school. Maybe you feel that bullying is just a normal part of school life. You might also think that face-to-face bullying is much worse than cyberbullying since the victims of real-world bullying have more difficulty escaping their tormentors, while a victim of cyberbullying can simply turn off the computer or block a bully on a social media platform.

Unfortunately, it's not that simple. And while the effects of real-world bullying behavior are not to be dismissed, the effects of cyberbullying can actually be much worse. As parents, it is up to you to understand the true impact of cyberbullying, to recognize a change in your child's behavior as a result of cyberbullying, and to find a way to help your child in a supportive manner.

In a real-world bullying situation, most incidents of bullying occur between the victim and a bully (or group of bullies) in school. These incidents can range from simple name-calling to more significant acts of bullying, such as rumor-spreading, harassment, threats, and incidents of physical harm. However, whereas victims of real-world bullying can be granted a reprieve when they go home, there simply is no escape from cyberbullying. It doesn't end when the school bell rings. It can continue at any time, throughout all hours of the night. It can come in the form of text messages, social media posts, chatroom messages, images and videos that have been altered, and many other digital forms.

Cyberbullying leaves little opportunity for victims to defend themselves. There are no teachers or parents to see what is happening and intervene to put a stop to it. Cyberbullying can also be anonymous, leaving the victim little recourse to even report the bully to an authority figure. And cyberbullying can showcase the incidents of bullying to hundreds, or potentially even thousands, within a short period of time using social media platforms.

If the victim does know who the bully is and chooses to block them on social media, the bully can simply create a new account. Or they can text, message, or use a friend's account. Kids today are extremely resourceful and savvy with technology. If they are intent on cyberbullying, there's not much a victim can do to stop them.

People do and say hurtful or demeaning things online that they would never say in person and if a cyberbully decides to spread rumours or share embarrassing photos on social media, the words or images could go viral, hitting the radar of many youngsters within minutes.

In essence, cyberbullying is more relentless, crueler, and more damaging than real-world bullying. It is also one of the most significant stressors in a young individual's life. And while children who are bullied often attempt to hide such events from their parents, there can be very noticeable changes in your child's behaviour if they are a continuous victim of cyberbullying.

There will be certain changes in behaviour which might not be readily apparent at first, but as time goes on, you may notice one or more of the following:

*   A drop in social behaviour- avoiding friends or social events.
*   Isolating his or herself in their room more than usual.
*   Becoming more quiet or withdrawn.
*   Finding it hard to concentrate on schoolwork.
*   Grades dropping.
*   Losing interest in activities that they normally enjoy.

* Skipping school or expressing a desire to skip school.
* Appearing angry when looking at their phone, tablet, or computer.
* Hiding their phone or computer screen from view.
* Avoiding using their phone.
* Using drugs or alcohol.
* Expressing dark thoughts or emotions.
* Talking about suicide.

If you think that some of these behavioural changes seem a bit extreme, such as thoughts of suicide, you should know that the relationship between bullying and suicide is a strong one. In some cases, bullying alone may not always be the sole cause. The child may already be experiencing feelings of depression or anxiety due to problems at home or a previous history of trauma.

if you recognize any of the signs described above, take the time to sit with your child and attempt to coax them to open up about any problems they are having in or out of school. By being supportive and understanding, you may aid your child in feeling as though they are not wholly alone.
Try to instill a sense of understanding that, as harsh and cruel as the bullying may be, the bullying is not a reflection of your child's worth, but rather it is more representative of the issues the bully may have in their own life.

Understandably, a child is not going to be very receptive to that train of thought, but that is not your only recourse. The first step is to make every attempt to adjust the privacy settings on your child's social media and chat accounts and to block any known cyberbullies.

Next, gather all evidence of cyberbullying, being sure to take screenshots, since many posts can be deleted. Report incidences of cyberbullying to the app or platform administrators, since cyberbullying often violates the terms of services.

With your evidence, you can also contact school administrators. Just because the incidents may not always happen at school is no reason the school administrators should not be made aware of the actions. Many schools have strict anti-bullying/cyberbullying policies. If cyberbullying contains any threats of physical violence, it can also be reported to your local police department.

Finally, find ways to help your child heal emotionally. You may need to engage the services of a mental health professional. Do not simply dismiss the effects of cyberbullying or consider them over if the cyberbullying stops. The effects can be long-lasting, and if the cyberbullying has been severe, it may take more than your kind words and advice to rectify the damage that has taken a toll.

Today's technology also comes with a number of parental controls to help safeguard kids from harmful or inappropriate online material. You can also avail yourself of third-party apps which offers protection from harmful content, as well as enables you to set screen time limits, monitor their online activity, or track their location with GPS. You can easily block your children from accidentally (or purposefully) viewing adult content while also ensuring they don't spend an unhealthy amount of time online.

Research and data collection are fundamental to understanding the trends and factors contributing to suicide. Data-driven insights can inform evidence-based policies and interventions, leading to more effective prevention efforts.

Addressing suicide necessitates collaboration between stakeholders at all levels. Governments, non-governmental organizations, mental health professionals, educators, and individuals must work hand in hand to create a society that values mental health and offers support to those in need.

In the digital age, suicide prevention requires an understanding of the impact of technology on mental health and well-being. By addressing cyberbullying, promoting digital well-being, harnessing technology for mental health support, and educating users about online risks, we can create a safer and more compassionate digital landscape. Together, we can leverage technology to enhance suicide prevention efforts and ensure that the digital age becomes a space of hope, support, and resilience for individuals in need.

Chapter 7

SUICIDE PREVENTION STRATEGIES

Suicide prevention is a collection of efforts to reduce the risk of suicide. It is often preventable and the efforts to prevent it may occur at the individual, relationship, community, and society level. Suicide is a serious public health problem that can have long-lasting effects on individuals, families, and communities. Preventing suicide requires strategies at all levels of society. This includes prevention and protective strategies for individuals, families, and communities. Suicide can be prevented by learning the warning signs, promoting prevention and resilience, and committing to social change.

Beyond direct interventions to stop an impending suicide, methods may include:

-Treating mental illness.
-Improving coping strategies of people who are at risk.
-Reducing risk factors for suicide, such as substance misuse, poverty and social vulnerability.
-Giving people hope for a better life after current problems are resolved.
-Calling a suicide hotline number.

General efforts include measures within the realms of medicine, mental health, and public health. Because protective factors such as social support and social engagement, as well as environmental risk factors such as access to lethal means, play a role in suicide, suicide is not solely a medical or mental-health issue. The following are some suicide prevention strategies:

Lethal-means reduction

This means reducing the odds that a person attempting suicide will use highly lethal means which is an important component of suicide prevention. This practice is also called "means restriction". It has been demonstrated that restricting lethal means can help reduce suicide rates, as delaying action until the desire to die has passed. In general, strong evidence supports the effectiveness of means restriction in preventing suicides. There is also strong evidence that restricted access at so-called suicide hotspots, such as bridges and cliffs, reduces suicides, whereas other interventions such as placing signs or increasing surveillance at these sites appears less effective.

One of the most famous historical examples of means reduction is that of coal gas in the United Kingdom. Until the 1950s, the most common means of suicide in the UK was poisoning by gas inhalation. In 1958, natural gas (virtually free of carbon monoxide) was introduced, and over the next decade, comprised over 50% of gas used. As carbon monoxide in gas decreased, suicides also decreased. The decrease was driven entirely by dramatic decreases in the number of suicides by carbon monoxide poisoning.

More so, in the United States, firearm access is associated with increased suicide completion. About 85% of suicide attempts with a gun result in death, while most other widely used suicide attempt methods result in death less than 5% of the time. Some researchers compared the number of suicides in state with the highest rates of gun ownership, to the number of suicides in states with the lowest rates of gun ownership. They found that men were 3.7 times more likely to die by firearm suicide and women were 7.9 times more likely to die by firearm suicide living in states with high rates of gun ownership. There was no difference in non-firearm suicides. Although restrictions on access to firearms have reduced firearm suicide rates in other countries, such restrictions are difficult in the diaspora.

Crisis hotline

As a suicide prevention initiative, organisations promote special telephones that connect to a crisis hotline, as well as a 24/7 crisis text line. Crisis hotlines connect a person in distress to either a volunteer or staff member. This may occur via telephone, online chat, or in person. Even though crisis hotlines are common, they have not been well studied. One study found a decrease in psychological pain, hopelessness, and desire to die from the beginning of the call through the next few weeks; however, the desire to die did not decrease long term.

Diet

About 50% of people who die of suicide have a mood disorder such as major depression. Sleep and diet may play a role in depression (major depressive disorder), and interventions in these areas may be an effective add-on to conventional methods. Vitamin B2, B6 and B12 deficiency may cause depression in females. Vitamin B12, for humans, is the only vitamin that must be sourced from animal-derived foods or from supplements. Only some archaea and bacteria can synthesize vitamin B12. Foods containing vitamin B12 include meat, clams, liver, fish, poultry, eggs, and dairy products. Many breakfast cereals are fortified with the vitamin. Natural sources of Vitamin B2 (riboflavin) include meat, fish and fowl, eggs, dairy products, green vegetables, mushrooms, and almonds.

Community-based programs

This involves screening and reducing risky behaviour through psychological resilience programs that promotes optimism and connectedness. Here, education about suicide, risk factors, warning signs, stigma related issues are made available through social campaigns. This in many ways would increasing the proficiency of health and welfare services at responding to people in need. e.g. sponsored training for helping professionals, increased access to community linkages, employing crisis counseling organizations etcetera.

Media guidelines

Recommendations around media reporting of suicide include not sensationalizing the event or attributing it to a single cause. It is also recommended that media messages include suicide prevention messages such as stories of hope and links to further resources. Particular care is recommended when a public figure or celebrity dies. It's not even recommended that some specific details or the location of the occurrence be given.

TV shows and news media may also be able to help prevent suicide by linking suicide with negative outcomes such as pain for the person who has attempted suicide and their survivors, conveying that the majority of people choose something other than suicide in order to solve their problems.

Medication

The medication lithium may be useful in certain situations to reduce the risk of suicide. Specifically it is effective at lowering the risk of suicide in those with bipolar disorder and major depressive disorder. Some antidepressant medications may increase suicidal ideation in some patients under certain conditions.

Counseling

There are multiple talking therapies that reduce suicidal thoughts and behaviours including dialectical behaviour therapy and cognitive behaviour therapy for suicide prevention (CBT-SP) which are adapted for adolescents who are at high risk for repeated suicide attempts. The brief intervention and contact technique developed by the World Health Organization recommends that specific skills be made available in the education system to prevent bullying and violence in and around the school.

Coping planning

Coping planning is a strengths-based intervention that aims to meet the needs of people who ask for help, including those experiencing suicidal ideation. By addressing why someone asks for help, the risk assessment and management stays on what the person needs, and the needs assessment focuses on the individual needs of each person. The coping planning approach to suicide prevention draws on the health-focused theory of coping. Coping is normalized as a normal and universal human response to unpleasant emotions, and interventions are considered a change continuum of low intensity (e.g., self-soothing) to high intensity support (e.g. professional help). By planning for coping, it supports people who are distressed and provides a sense of belongingness and resilience in treatment of illness. A good coping planning strategically develops resilience and regulates strengths.

The traditional approach has been to identify the risk factors that increase suicide or self-harm, though meta-analysis studies suggest that suicide risk assessment might not be useful and recommend immediate hospitalization of the person with suicidal feelings as the healthy choice. In 2001, the U.S. Department of Health and Human Services, published the National Strategy for Suicide Prevention, establishing a framework for suicide prevention in the U.S. The document, and its 2012 revision, calls for a public health approach to suicide prevention, focusing on identifying patterns of suicide and suicidal ideation throughout a group or population (as opposed to exploring the history and health conditions that could lead to suicide in a single individual). The ability to recognize warning signs of suicide allows individuals who may be concerned about someone they know to direct them to help.

Suicide gesture and suicidal desire (a vague wish for death without any actual intent to kill oneself) are potentially self-injurious behaviors that a person may use to attain some other ends, like to seek help, punish others, or to receive attention. This behaviour has the potential to aid an individual's capability for suicide and can be considered as a suicide warning, when the person shows intent through verbal and behavioral signs.

Suicide prevention strategies focus on reducing the risk factors and intervening strategically to reduce the level of risk. Risk and protective factors unique to the individual can be assessed by a qualified mental health professional. Some of the specific strategies used to address are:

a)Crisis intervention.

b)Structured counseling and psychotherapy.

c)Hospitalization for those with low adherence to collaboration for help and those who require monitoring and secondary symptom treatment.

d)Supportive therapy like substance abuse treatment, Psychotropic medication, Family psychoeducation and Access to emergency phone call care with emergency rooms, suicide prevention hotlines, etc.

e)Restricting access to lethality of suicide means through policies and laws.

f)Creating and using crisis cards, an easy-to-read uncluttered card that describes a list of activities one should follow in crisis until the positive behaviour responses settles in the personality.

g)Person-centered life skills training. e.g., Problem solving.

h)Registering with support groups like Alcoholics Anonymous, Suicide Bereavement Support Group, a religious group with flow rituals, etc.

i)Therapeutic recreational therapy that improves mood.

j)Motivating self-care activities like physical exercises and meditative relaxation.

Suicide prevention must be responsive to the diverse needs of at-risk populations. Tailored approaches that address the unique challenges faced by LGBTQ+ individuals, veterans, Indigenous peoples, youth, older adults, racial and ethnic minorities, people with disabilities, those with substance use disorders, and confined individuals are essential in saving lives. By understanding the specific risk factors and promoting targeted interventions, we can create a more equitable and inclusive suicide prevention strategy that saves lives and fosters resilience in all segments of society. Together, we can work towards a future where no one is left behind in the fight against suicide, and every life is valued and protected.

Suicide prevention demands a comprehensive and compassionate approach that involves individuals, communities, healthcare professionals, and policymakers. By implementing education, training, means restriction, crisis support, and fostering resilience, we can create a society where suicide is preventable, and mental health support is readily available. Together, we must prioritize suicide prevention and work towards a future where compassion, empathy, and understanding form the bedrock upon which lives are saved, and hope is restored.

Chapter 8

THE AFTERMATH
OF SUICIDE

The aftermath of a suicide attempt or loss is a deeply challenging and painful experience for individuals, families, and communities. Postvention, the support provided after a suicide-related event, is crucial in promoting healing, reducing the risk of further incidents, and offering comfort to those affected.

After a suicide attempt or loss, immediate support is essential. Crisis counselors, mental health professionals, and trained volunteers should be available to offer comfort, empathy, and guidance during this critical period. The emotional impact of a suicide attempt or loss can be overwhelming. Grief, guilt, anger, and confusion are common reactions. Creating safe spaces for individuals to express their feelings and providing grief counseling can facilitate the healing process. Individuals who have survived a suicide attempt require specialized care and support. Addressing the underlying mental health issues and providing a comprehensive treatment plan is vital in reducing the risk of future attempts.

Survivors of suicide loss may experience complicated grief, characterized by intense emotions and difficulty in coping with the loss. Bereavement support groups and counseling can offer solace and understanding during this difficult time. In fact, the impact of suicide is not limited to immediate family members. Entire communities can experience grief and trauma. Community healing events and educational initiatives can help destigmatize suicide and promote understanding and empathy.

Through my foundation- **"Wise Kuku Foundation"** that caters to counselling young persons who survived suicide attempts, I have been in touch with quite a number of them. One that stood out for me was a teenager who was quite lovable in his community but still decided to take their own life due to the rejection he faced from family.

A shock wave went through the entire community and even his family struggled to understand what had happened, and kept asking the question "How could something like this happen?" That was a question I didn't need to ask, because some years ago, I, too, had attempted suicide.

It didn't make the grief any less painful, of course. I still had countless moments of self-blame, confusion, and despair but it wasn't as incomprehensible as it was to everyone else, because it was a struggle I knew too well. My experience on "both sides" became a blessing in disguise. When young people asked me how a suicide attempt could happen, I am able to answer and as I field their questions, I see that I could heal and empathize with them.

While I can't speak for every person who has struggled with suicidal thoughts, I've spoken to enough survivors to know there are commonalities in how we've felt about the experience. I want to share what those commonalities are in the hopes that if you've survived a loss like this, you might be able to find some comfort in hearing from someone who's been there.

Suicide is more complex than a 'decision'. People who attempt suicide aren't always convinced it's the only option. It's more often that they have exhausted their emotional reserves to continue pursuing those options. It is, in many ways, the ultimate state of burnout which doesn't happen overnight, either. In order to attempt suicide, a person has to be in the neurological state where they can override their own survival instincts. He has to have reached a point where he feels the capacity for emotional pain has outweighed the amount of time he is able to wait for relief, at the same moment when he has access to the means to end his life. Suicide is a tragic outcome of extraordinary circumstances that, in reality, many people can't control except by the power of God.

Suicidal thoughts, once they snowball, can become an avalanche that drowns out the part of us that would otherwise choose differently. It's not that we aren't conflicted, so much as the suicidal thoughts are so incredibly loud. This is also why some of us (often unconsciously) sabotage our own attempts. We might choose a time or place when it's possible that we'll be discovered. We might drop hints about our mental state that are nearly undetectable to others. We might choose a method that isn't reliable. Even for those who meticulously planned and appeared very committed to killing themselves, they are, in a way, sabotaging themselves. The longer we take to plan, the more we leave open the possibility of an intervention or slipup.

We desperately want peace and ease, which is really the only thing we are sure of. A suicide attempt doesn't reflect how we felt about our life, our potential, or about you, at least, not as much as it reflects our state of mind in the moment when we attempted.

Suicide attempts are often as much an emotional event as they are a neurological one. When I speak to other attempt survivors, many of us share the same feeling: We didn't want to hurt our loved ones, but that tunnel vision and state of acute pain, along with the sense that we're a burden on those we care about, can override our judgment.

Sometimes, a suicide attempt doesn't necessarily mean someone didn't believe they were loved. It doesn't mean your loved one didn't know you cared or believed they wouldn't get the unconditional acceptance and care that you (without a doubt) had to offer. Sadly, love is not enough to keep someone here, if it were, we would see much fewer deaths by suicide but I can tell you that love makes our time here on earth more meaningful. I can also say it sustains in many dark moments.

Before my attempt, I wanted nothing more than to get better and be strong enough to stay. But as the walls closed in on me, I stopped believing I could. Your loved one's suicide attempt says nothing about how much you loved them, nor how much they loved you.

If you have ever lost someone to suicide, its normal to want to blame yourself. It's easy to fall down the rabbit hole of rumination, wondering what you could've done differently. It's gut-wrenching but also, in some ways, comforting, because it deludes you into thinking that you might have had some kind of control over the outcome. Wouldn't the world feel so much safer if it were possible to save everyone we loved? To spare them from their suffering with the right words, the right decisions? That, through sheer force of will, we could save everyone. Or at the very least, the people we can't imagine our lives without.

I believed that for a long time. I really did. I've written publicly about mental health and suicide for the last five years, and I truly believed that, if someone I loved was in trouble, they would know, without question, they could call me.

But when a pot of water is on the gas, even if you turn up the flame, you aren't responsible for when the water boils. If left on the burner long enough, it was always going to come to a boil. Our mental health system is supposed to provide a safety net that takes that pot off the burner so that, no matter what happens with the flame, it never gets to a fever pitch and boils over.

You aren't responsible for that systemic failure, no matter what mistakes you did or didn't make. You were failed, too, because you were made to feel responsible for your loved one's life, which is much too heavy a responsibility for any person to carry. You're not a crisis professional, and even if you are, you're not perfect. You're only human.

I've come to realise that grief is a powerful teacher. It's challenged me continually to recommit to living a purposeful life. To give my heart away freely and readily, to speak truth to power, and most importantly, to let the life I lead be a living dedication to young people my story could inpire.

I've learned to live alongside my grief, to let it transform me as radically as possible. Each moment I find the strength to do what's right, to be brave and relentless in fighting for a more just world, or to simply let myself laugh without feeling self-conscious, I become the living and breathing altar for God to share his compassion, courage, joy with others.

I can tell you, both as a survivor of loss and of an attempt, that life is unquestionably precious and I believe that more fiercely than I ever have before. You're still here. And whatever the reason might be, you still have the chance to do something extraordinary with this life.

My greatest wish for you, and for anyone who's grieving, is to know that your pain doesn't have to consume you. Let it be your compass that leads you to new and exciting places. Let it bring you closer to your purpose. Let it remind you of how precious your own being is.

You're part of a good legacy; fight for your own life the way you so desperately wish you could fight for others.

Chapter 9

THE WAY FORWARD

In the journey to prevent suicide, we have witnessed the power of unity, compassion, and collective action. The efforts of individuals, communities, organizations, and governments have made a profound impact on suicide prevention worldwide. As we reflect on the knowledge and strategies presented in this book, we reaffirm our commitment to building a world united for suicide prevention.

Through education and awareness, we have dismantled the barriers of stigma and replaced ignorance with understanding. We have learned to recognize the warning signs of suicide and how to offer support to those in need. Together, we have fostered resilience in vulnerable populations, acknowledging that every life is valuable and worth protecting.

In the face of adversity, we have shown the strength of human spirit by providing immediate support during crises and advocating for mental health services for all. We have understood that suicide prevention knows no boundaries, and we have reached across cultures and nations to learn from one another and share best practices.

The road to a suicide-free world is long, and the journey is ongoing. We must continue to push for progress, engage in research and data collection, and refine our approaches to better serve those at risk. We must be vigilant in our efforts to protect the most vulnerable and work together to address the root causes of suicide.

In every corner of the globe, we extend our hand in solidarity to those who have lost loved ones to suicide, offering comfort and support. To those who have survived suicide attempts, we offer hope and a promise that healing is possible. Together, we stand as a global community, bound by a shared commitment to suicide prevention and mental well-being.

As we conclude, let us remember that every life saved is a testament to the power of compassion and human connection. We carry this torch forward, lighting the way for a future where suicide is a thing of the past. United, we will prevail in the fight against suicide, making the world a safer, more caring, and resilient place for all.

May this book be a testament to the collective determination to prevent suicide and a source of inspiration for generations to come. Let us continue to work hand in hand, driven by hope, love, and the unwavering belief that together, we can make a difference.

The journey continues, and together, we will create a world united for suicide prevention.

"United We Stand, United We Prevent."

HOW I FOUGHT — DEPRESSION — HANDS DOWN

Depression and suicide work hand in hand to eat up the soul of God's creation and I must confess that each day there's a battle raging for your soul. Our emotions are a spiritual battleground, and as a child of God, we are not immune to Satan's attacks. In fact, the more you live for Christ, the more of a threat you become to the devil. The bible says in Ephesians 6:12:

"For we do not wrestle against flesh and blood, but against the rulers, against the authorities, against the cosmic powers over this present darkness, against the spiritual forces of evil in the heavenly places."

When Satan or circumstances bring you sadness, don't question your salvation or your relationship with God like the enemy wants. Instead, acknowledge his evil schemes and equip yourself to fight back with the word of God. Once you have received Christ and are a child of God, Satan will try to use all his diabolical techniques to thwart, hinder and defeat you.

Truth be told, we don't always feel happy or feel like smiling. On days when happiness seems in short supply, lean into joy. Pick up the Bible to read and connect with the words inspired by God Himself. Then you will begin to feel differently from within despite your situation. You will be able to live Philippians 4:4 everyday which says, "rejoice in the Lord always; again I will say, rejoice."

Meanwhile, we know Jesus is our only hope. However, we might not wake up every morning eager to dig into the Bible, pray to our Father and sing His praises. When you're in the depths of depression, talking to God may be the last thing you feel like doing and you may eventually succumb to doing the wrong thing like I did. After I discovered that my confidant had become pregnant for me, I was shattered. I had no rest until I decided to confess my sins. My parents were highly disappointed in me. They gave me the option to terminate the pregnancy and dissociate from the lady if I wanted their trust back. I was in a dilemma and knew it wasn't right to kill a soul. Then he sent me out of the house and told me to shoulder my new family responsibilities. I started doubting my blood ties with my family of orientation.

Then I stumbled on a radio broadcast where the preacher mentioned about the story of the prodigal son in Luke 15:11-32. This made me get connected to some spiritual persons who counseled me to move closer to God. I located a Bible-believing church where I was welcomed with open arms. I was introduced to their discipleship programme where they taught me the true word of God. These words keep ringing in my head every time Satan tries to remind me of my past. God continued to pursue me and cling on to me even when I wasn't clinging to Him or even looking for Him. I no longer need to fake happiness because I now have the real joy.

I used to feel ashamed by my struggles that I wasn't good enough because of them. Now, I am reminded that my trials make Christ's sacrifice on the cross that much more beautiful and meaningful to me.

To the glory of God today, I have a beautiful family. Like David who was rejected but became a King and Joseph a slave boy who later became a Prime minister in a foreign land, I have come to realise that God saw me through my suicide journey and put people along my path to prepare me ahead of young people who will have the same experience.

If you're going through issues, no one can really help except God. He will direct people to your path to help you. Kindly reach out to us at the **"Wise Kuku Youth Development Foundation"** to walk you through your healing process as God enables us.